Hi lovely! If you enjoyed this book, it would really mean a lot if you could leave a review. Thank you! :)

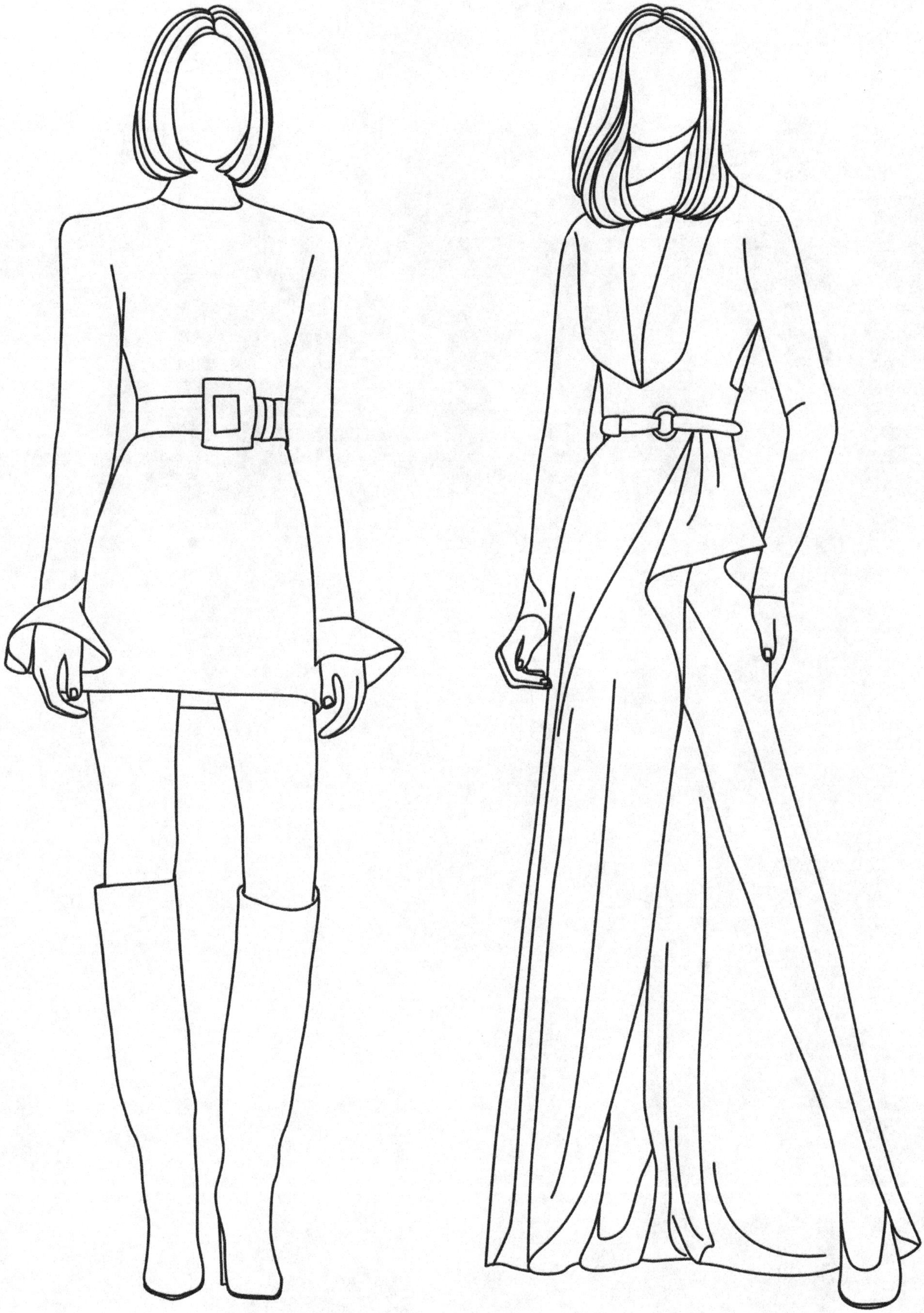

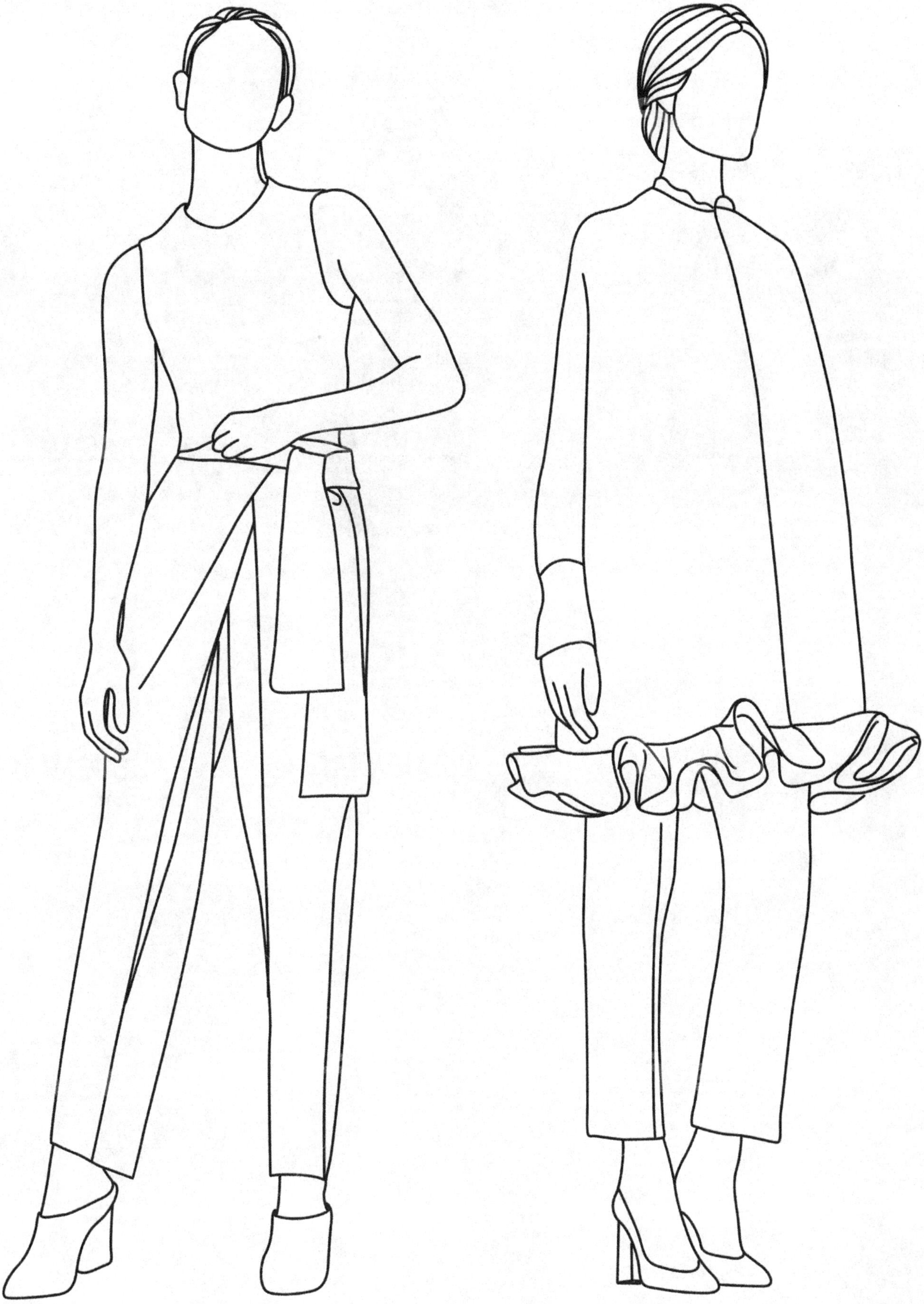

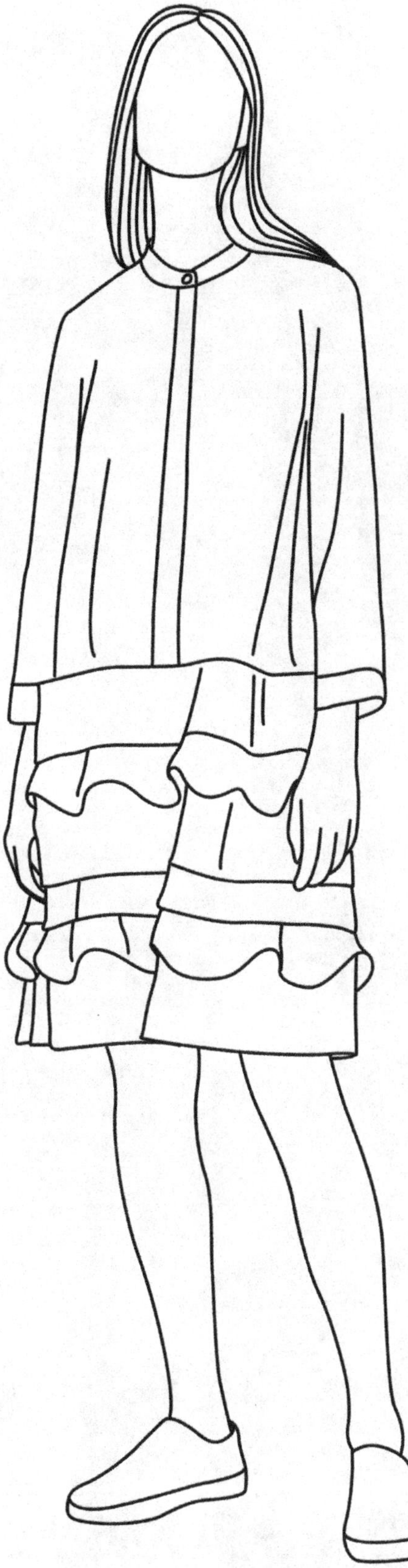

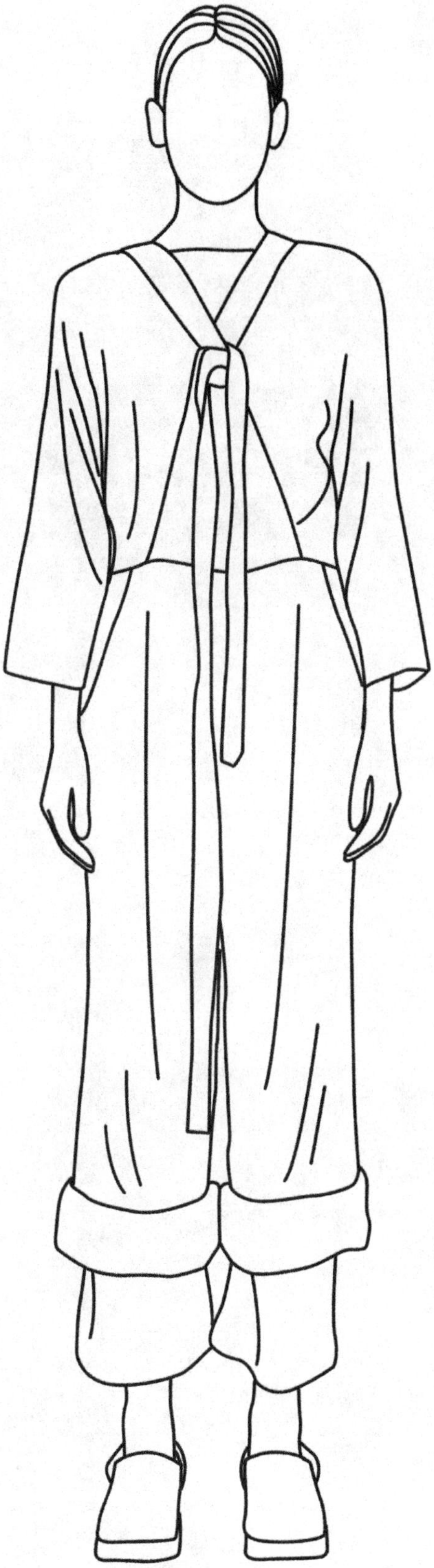

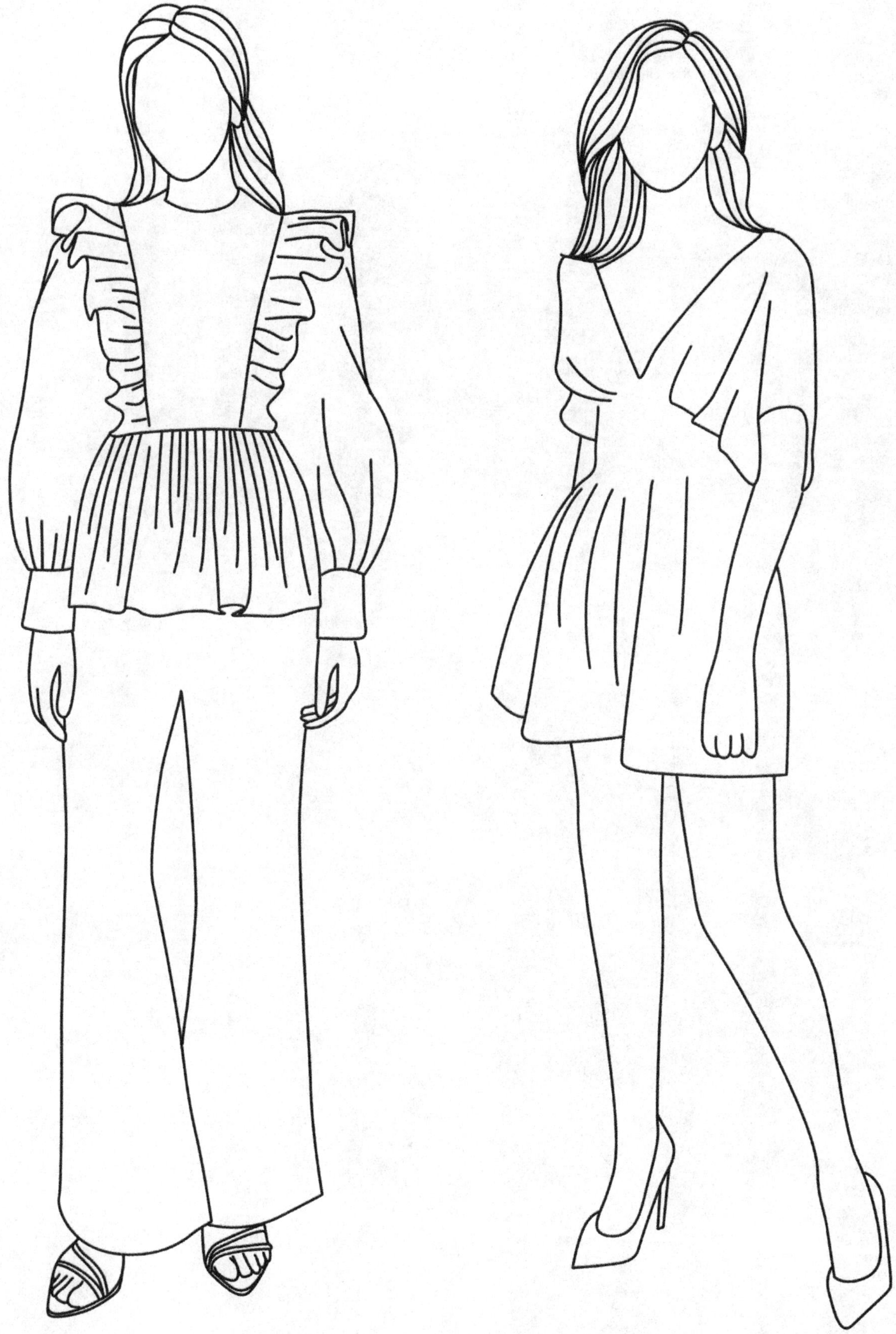

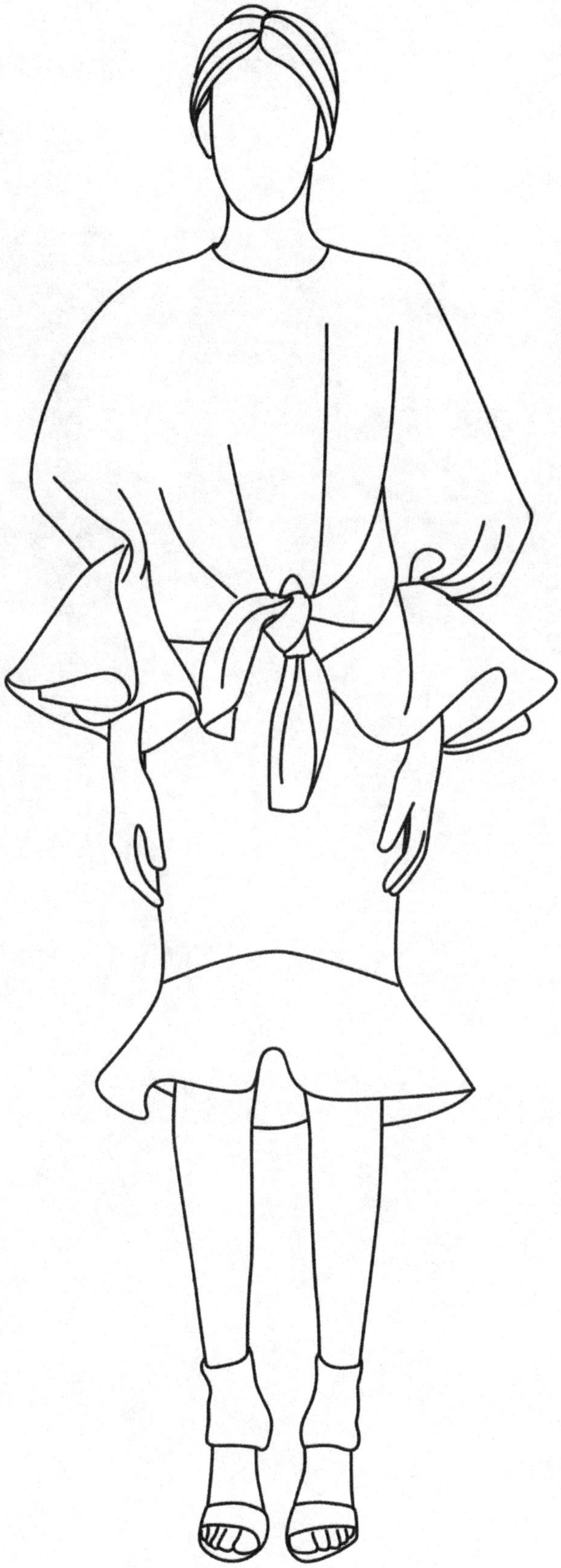

Made in the USA
Las Vegas, NV
03 October 2024

96223078R00057